Little Pebble™

Holidays Around the World

Diwali

by Lisa J. Amstutz

CAPSTONE PRESS
a capstone imprint

Little Pebble is published by Capstone Press,
1710 Roe Crest Drive, North Mankato, Minnesota 56003
www.mycapstone.com

Library of Congress Cataloging-in-Publication Data
Library of Congress Cataloging-in-Publication data is available on the Library
of Congress website.
ISBN 978-1-5157-4853-3 (library binding)
ISBN 978-1-5157-4859-5 (paperback)
ISBN 978-1-5157-4877-9 (eBook PDF)
Summary: Explains how people prepare for and celebrate the holiday of Diwali.

Editorial Credits
Jill Kalz, editor; Julie Peters, designer; Pam Mitsakos, media researcher;
Steve Walker, production specialist

Photo Credits
Getty Images: Hemant Mehta, 13; iStockphoto: Hasilyus, 21; Shutterstock: Dipak
Shelare, 7, India Picture, 9, 17, 19, indianstockimages, cover, jamesteohart, 1,
22, 24, back cover, phive, 16, Shiny Designer, 3, Sirin_bird, design element,
stocksolutions, 15, szefei, 14, TheFinalMiracle, 5; Thinkstock: WebSubstance, 11

Printed and bound in China.
PO7884LEOS17

Table of Contents

What Is Diwali?

Look at all the lights!

Diwali is here!

Diwali is in October or November. This holiday lasts five days.

It is a time to pray
and give thanks.

Getting Ready

People clean their homes.
They buy new clothes. They
paint their hands and feet.

11

Diwali Begins

Some people give gifts.

They share sweets.

Families have a feast.

They talk and have fun.

Diyas glow. They welcome the gods. They show that good wins over evil.

See the pretty art?

Rangoli is made

of sand, rice, or flowers.

People put it by the door.

Pop! Boom! Fireworks light the sky. Happy Diwali!

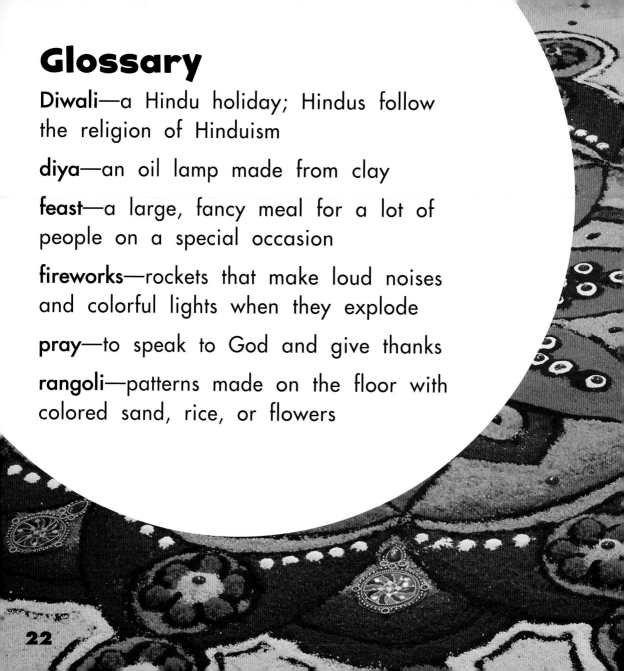

Glossary

Diwali—a Hindu holiday; Hindus follow the religion of Hinduism

diya—an oil lamp made from clay

feast—a large, fancy meal for a lot of people on a special occasion

fireworks—rockets that make loud noises and colorful lights when they explode

pray—to speak to God and give thanks

rangoli—patterns made on the floor with colored sand, rice, or flowers

Read More

Dickmann, Nancy. *Diwali*. Holidays and Festivals. Chicago: Heinemann Library, 2011.

Murray, Julie. *Diwali*. Holidays. Edina, Minn.: ABDO Publishing Company, 2014.

Pettiford, Rebecca. *Diwali*. Holidays. Minneapolis: Bullfrog Books, 2015.

Internet Sites

FactHound offers a safe, fun way to find Internet sites related to this book. All of the sites on FactHound have been researched by our staff.

Here's all you do:
Visit *www.facthound.com*
Type in this code: 9781515748533

Super-cool stuff!

Check out projects, games and lots more at
www.capstonekids.com

Critical Thinking Using the Common Core

1. Name three things people may do during Diwali. (Key Ideas and Details)

2. Diyas do two important things. What are they? (Key Ideas and Details)

Index